BOOK *of* CHANGES

BOOK *of* CHANGES

POEMS

Karen Holden

Foreword by
Stephen Mitchell

North Atlantic Books
Berkeley, California

Book of Changes

Published by
North Atlantic Books
P.O. Box 12327
Berkeley, California 94712

www.northatlanticbooks.com

Cover painting by Karen Holden
Chinese calligraphy by Ling Po
Cover and book design by Legacy Media, Inc.

Printed in the United States of America.

Book of Changes is sponsored by the Society for the Study of Native
Arts and Sciences, a nonprofit educational corporation whose goals
are to develop an educational and crosscultural perspective linking
various scientific, social, and artistic fields; to nurture a holistic view
of arts, sciences, humanities, and healing; and to publish and dis-
tribute literature on the relationship of mind, body, and nature.

Library of Congress Cataloging-in-Publication Data
Holden, Karen, 1955–
    Book of Changes / Karen Holden.
        p.   cm.
    ISBN 1-55643-263-1 (paperback)
    1. I Ching—Poetry.   2. Philosophy, Chinese—Poetry.   I. Title.
    PS3558.0347752B66   1998
    811'.54—dc21   97-47265
                                                        CIP

2   3   4   5   6   7   8   9 / 05   04   03   02   01

This book is for the Sages, seen and unseen,
who made it possible
And for Eric, who is among them

CONTENTS

FOREWORD

The poems of Karen Holden's *Book of Changes* can be read in two ways: by themselves or in conjunction with the texts of the *I Ching*. They are a pleasure on their own, and there are many things to admire about them: their honesty and vulnerability, the freshness of their language, their sensuality, their intimacy with the vivid world of gardens.

But because Karen Holden uses the *I Ching* as her organizing principle, her book is a dialogue between the impersonal and the very personal. Each poem is not only itself: it is joined to one of the sixty-four hexagrams like a melody to a running bass. This fusion gives the poem a depth beyond its occasion. And since each poem has its place within the ancient pattern, there is a subtle narrative movement that makes the book as a whole more than a collection of separate pieces. It is a narrative that strings one woman's life across the turning points of the cosmos: the ups and downs, the strengths and weaknesses, the joys and sorrows, the seasons as they vanish and return, the ebb and flow of the stars.

Stephen Mitchell

ACKNOWLEDGMENTS

It is impossible to thank all the people who made this book possible, for it would be everyone who has been a part of my life: my family, friends, teachers and students, and, as Robert Duncan said "those unknown, alike in soul."

Particular thanks to Michael Ventura and Bill Mohr for reading and commenting upon early drafts, to Ling Po for his beautiful calligraphy, and to Victor who scanned it; to Mary Wright for her encouragement and ever-present ear, to Paula, Bernard, MaryLee, Amy and all the other poets who grace my life; to Sandra for being my oldest friend, to Steve for his devilish laugh, to Mark, Jackie and of course, everyone at Taliesin, to Eric for everything; to the wonderful souls at North Atlantic Books: Richard, Anastasia, Ayelet, and especially Susan, who treated me with such respect and yes, I will say it, love, that the publishing process was a dream — they believed in this book and let me know it.

Thanks also, to the following magazines and anthologies in which a number of these poems first appeared (some without title): *Poetry/LA*: "And Then," "Beach," "Dungeness, Yesterday," "Following," "What the Body Gives Us"; *Invocation L.A.*: "Preponderance of the Small," "The Family," "Coming to Meet"; *Sculpture Gardens Review*: "Dispersion [Dissolution]," "But My Name is Allan."

All quotes not credited are quoted directly or adapted from the *I Ching* or *Book of Changes,* Richard Wilhelm & Cary Baynes translation, Bollingen/Princeton University Press, 1950.

INTRODUCTION

The *I Ching* or *Book of Changes* is an ancient Chinese oracle and philosophical text. In its current form it is made up of 64 hexagrams with extensive commentary. It may have begun as a yes/no oracle, and was used as a natural almanac as well as a source of divination. Legend traces the oracle back to Fu Hsi in the 3rd millennium B.C.

It has been edited, rearranged and commented upon by rulers and scholars since then. It is believed that King Wen, who founded the Zhou Dynasty (1150–249 B.C.) wrote extensively on the meanings of the hexagrams, and his son the Duke of Zhou completed the work by writing commentaries on each of the lines within the hexagrams. Lao Tzu, Chuang Tzu, Mencius, were all influenced by the *I Ching,* and subsequently influenced the text through their own writings. Confucius (551–479 B.C.) made a large contribution to our understanding of the text by writing a series of commentaries about the hexagrams and their individual lines. Confucius' followers also revised and shaped the text. New archaeological discoveries are changing what we know about the history and authorship of the I Ching. What is remarkable about the book, regardless of its origins, is its development over the centuries as an interactive product of multiple authors.

The *I Ching* can be used as a philosophical text, or to

predict the future, as well as to give insight into a current situation. To access the oracle, one asks a particular question, then throws three coins six times (or divides 50 yarrow sticks in a particular manner). The combination of numbers creates the hexagrams; one then reads the commentaries to gain understanding of the situation posed in the question. The text of the *I Ching* relies on the concept of "the great reversal": the Yin and Yang. It is based on the idea that everything is constantly changing from dark to light, negative to positive, creative to receptive. When one is able to understand the nature of the moment, and accept the inviolable law of change, one will meet with success in his or her endeavors. The book is also founded on a belief in destiny, and working in concert with fate to achieve proper balance and ease of movement in one's life.

I have had an ongoing relationship with the *I Ching* since 1986. I find the book to be a comfort, a cudgel, and a source of great insight. My interest in it has led me to read numerous other works about the book in particular and Chinese philosophy in general. I am involved in the same struggle with myself and the world we all are; and the *Book of Changes* helps me gain clarity and perspective at those times I need it most. I am eternally grateful to Richard Wilhelm for his translation of the text from Chinese and to Cary Baynes for the translation to English. Although I use other translations, and secondary sources, I rely most heavily on Wilhelm/Baynes — it still speaks to me most poetically.

I also thank Carl Jung, a proponent of the *I Ching*

who helped make it readily available in the west, Alyn who gave me his father's book and Peter who showed me how to use it.

The poems in my *Book of Changes* were inspired, informed or somehow shaped by my interactions with the *I Ching* over the years. Some of them sprang directly from my work with the text. Others had a life of their own and found their way into a pairing with a particular hexagram when I was compiling this book. Certain hexagrams seemed to want to hold, gobble and grab many poems. Others seemed to repel all. I would find myself driving down a boulevard reassessing a particular pairing, feeling wobbly about a certain poem, until finally everything fell into place, and I breathed an 'of course' about each poem's part in the whole. My desire is that the book communicate a life, a sensibility, and a view that I myself *discovered* in doing this work.

Lao Tzu, in Stephen Mitchell's translation of the *Tao Te Ching* (a book I keep with me always) says, "A good artist lets his intuition lead him wherever it wants." This has been my goal — to be led into this work and be enriched by it. And so I have.

Karen Holden
Los Angeles
Winter Solstice 1996

BOOK *of* CHANGES

1
CH'IEN
The Creative

乾

Primal power. Light-giving, conceived in motion, active, and of the spirit. This is the energy of Heaven, within which all things manifest and persist in time.

The Creative

She is a light. She is a flame. And how disturbed we are when the flame begins to flicker. And don't we hurry to shut the window, to protect her from the draft. She is a beacon and rocky shore that we long to crash into. The precipice. We force our bodies away from the pinhole in the door through which we see a rib of light, but which allows us no vision of what is inside. She is movement, a turning wand, the end of the road with no home, a voice in an empty subway — nobody there and Sunday morning without the newspaper. And how we grind our teeth at the empty doorstep, don't we, and we know we are helpless now that Sunday has begun and we are stranded with ourselves and the teeming light that makes us squint. And where is she? She is the light.

2

K'UN

≡≡
≡≡
≡≡

The Receptive

Dark, yielding, devoted, accepting of guidance.
The image here is of earth's ability to nourish
all living things as they willingly surrender to
the nature of the world.

坤

The Receptive

Each breast becomes a small bird as I cup it in my
hand. I can feel its beating through my fingertips
though my hands no longer belong to me. I am the
body of the world embracing my own sad rhythm, such
joy the stillness makes. Borders are broken, laughter
spills between continents, the delicate skin of eyelid.
I am wet, amphibian, fluttering like small wings. The
long bone of leg stretches into its full length, shakes out
of bend. It is lovely in this garden. Be still now, long
only to be that open.

3
CHUN

Difficulty at the Beginning

*It is through the meeting of Heaven and
Earth that individuals are born; and this birth
is replete with difficulties. It is only through
struggle that we finally attain form.*

Difficulty at the Beginning

I sleep folded, as if I had no bones;
my hands so bent and flattened in sharp
downward curve to my chest that I wake
up numb. My knees lifted, ankles crossed,
feet curled, as if I was made of strips
of paper, or green bamboo. My shoulders
curve inward so far I walk with a slump,
the knobby human knuckles of my spine
grind and shift as if they remember
the black fluid body they once were and the
brief, ventilated life of dark and fragrant
pleasure. I can imagine the quick movements
from flower to flower through air as fine
as hair and no sleep until death. Each
morning still, it is as if I emerge from
some gray spun cocoon formed from strands
of my own being, and fight my way through
that same fine air; knowing, flexing, merely
waiting for my wings to dry.

4
MENG
Youthful Folly

Here, the imagination becomes a web;
and once one is caught in it, one is blind to
everything but unreal fantasy. This is the
nature of youth, a lack of experience that can
lead to humiliation.

Youthful Folly

the places he touches her. there. and how the light falls
across the bed, lighting the hairs on his arm, turning
them the color of sand. his smell. the way his hair curls
longer behind his left ear and the woven wish bracelet he
tied to his wrist in guatemala, dirty now and almost
worn off. how he sleeps like a child with his mouth
open, wetting the pillow; his fingers curling and
uncurling, clutching. he is golden as the sun slants even
more through the thin paper blind, golden, and it makes
her lose her breath that instant to realize she doesn't
care about all that. doesn't even care about his wet
finger running the length of her spine, or her tongue
tracing the vein in his arm. doesn't care about his
hands, with their broad fingers and flat wrists, the
muscled arms or the gift of morning he gives each time
his eyes open the color of summer. doesn't care about all
that. only his mouth, which says 'forever' even though
he doesn't mean it.

5
HSU

≡ ≡
≡ ≡
≡≡≡
≡≡≡

Waiting (Nourishment)
*"All beings have need of nourishment from
above. But the gift of food comes in its own
time, and for this one must wait."*

Waiting

How could I be sad in winter? All day I have the
persimmon. As day unfolds after bleak day, the soft
hearted fruit goes clear, a flame set against the brown
and mauve and sop of this endless season. We pluck
three or four each day until finally, in a fit at the end of
January, they all ripen at once; bright and jellied on the
branches that appear too slender to hold their weight.
Then my husband climbs his ladder and fills three
boxes; packs them skin to skin, carefully, like those
Christmas fruits we received each year as kids — round
swelling things made square by the pressure of
cardboard. I stick them in the freezer and imagine
spooning out the sweet icy flesh on the first eighty
degree day; a warming thought, and bracing. For now I
am caught between two fires; the bright blaze behind the
glass of the wood-stove, and out the window, one last
vibrant persimmon; too high to reach, not ready to fall.

6
SUNG

Conflict

The upper trigram, whose image is heaven, has an upward movement; the lower trigram, water, in accordance with its nature, tends downward. Thus the two halves move away from each other, giving rise to the idea of conflict.

Here we have someone who has carried a conflict to the bitter end and has triumphed. He is granted a decoration, but his happiness does not last. He is attacked again and again, and the result is conflict without end.

No Fallen Angel

See,
what we forget about Lucifer
is the underside of his wings,
that gold
God's hand prints on his chest,
his sad green eyes
and pallor.

How could a father forsake
such a child?
Why fear Satan?
He learned his fury from God.

7
SHIH

The Army

"Game is in the field — it has left its usual haunts in the forest ..."

The raw power of danger within, which can only be tempered by obedience without; such is an army, which must listen for command and follow.

A Life of Their Own

My dreams are like horses these days; full bodies
running by hot and sweat slicked before I can catch
them, over the crest before I can describe them.
They have a life of their own. I can't be sure they
are my horses; perhaps they've escaped from some
neighboring farm, or are wild, having hidden in the
trees and valleys for a long time before finally
breaking loose across the plains of my sleep.
They elude me, and it is just as well. For I have
lost my rope and halter, and am weaving, wild
myself, and packless, through my own unknown terrain;
no desire to capture, and only the invisible movement,
the muscles of God, leading me on.

8
PI

Holding Together [Union]
*We must unite with others; this is what
enriches the world. But in order not to lose
oneself, an enduring union should be based on
natural affinity and sanctioned from above.*

比

Natural

You are as natural to me
as the new moon hanging orange
in the city brown sky
as natural as night work
on the freeway, February rain
I look at you and see
suburban streets swelling
dark with rainwater
rushing the trash filled sewers
a river of cars and debris, metal
not a pretty power, but formidable
and your own
You are as natural as traffic
noise, constant and thick
as natural as heat
on the sidewalk, the mucky air
each staunch, vigorous palm tree
growing growing in a place
it does not belong
You are as natural as my two hands
on the steering wheel of a car
not the life I imagined
but formidable, and my own.

9

HSIAO CH'U

The Taming Power of the Small
*Wind sweeps the sky, but cannot
gather enough clouds to make rain. The
Creative is held in check for the time being by
a weak element. Although success is possible,
the time is not ripe for the release of built up
tensions.*

Electrical Storm

The sky deepens in the North, deepens to indigo. In the
West a rainbow shoots straight up from the ground, out
of the mountains; from the road it was a ball of color
the lightning cut. The clouds shift from long pink
shorelines to gray masses to white curls; fingers that
keep twining in on themselves. There are holes in the
clouds where the blue is turquoise, where it is ice, where
it's almost teal. The South is a yellow bruise. A salmon
ribbon lays across the mountain crest, light shoots from
cloud to cloud, it rains only far in the distance.
A western storm — there is nothing else like it; the way
it roils up the energy in a space, kinks time, shifts
perspective, mesmerizes, then drops. There is no way to
write this so I kneel in the gravel alongside the road,
kneel and bow to the wind that whips in a circle, cuts
the yellow grass and makes the neon campground sign
flicker. A teepee makes a bouquet of sticks against the
sky.
The flashes come in waves now rather than lines, I can
feel them in my bones. They seem to emanate from the

ground and I believe this; I believe that what seems to be sky is ground and what was once ground has dissolved into a feeling not yet slippery as rain.

Bill Davis thinks I am European, and out of campsites, offers me the teepee on this stormy night. He wears a turquoise necklace and a cowboy hat. He is excessive, polite and uses my name a lot; he has a good handshake. Storms do things to people — shift some subtle balance; cause them to rent out their advertising teepee to a broken woman on the road. A woman waiting for rain. The clouds are dishcloths in the wind, the East is lilac, periwinkle, salmon and clear skim milk; looks like swept sand and raked gravel, like caves. The teepee has a dirt floor and I sleep on it. The sky flashes white.

Oh, did I tell you? I woke at two a.m. covered in ants; had to get up and drive on.

10
LU

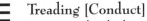

Treading [Conduct]

A Sage is lonely, but is not bound by social convention. He simply follows — is true to himself and makes no demands on people. He neither seeks nor is enticed by worldly goals. Thus, he does not challenge fate and is free.

Treading

slanting as it does late afternoon across the brim of a building peeling with smog and age it creates triangles that reflect the road work sign shows the clouds to be even more gray underneath and whiter against the blue pulled as they are like cotton yes and the sheen on the temple of the man moving down the street hunched over in the dark jacket his shoulder almost touching the wall the thin film of sweat or oil that gives his face a polished look contrasts the dirty polyester of his too short tan trousers and the shoes one lace missing full of holes he has no reason to see me here contemplating light at the last coffee break of everybody's day has no reason which doesn't stop him but neither does it make him go.

11
TA'I

Peace

*"This hexagram denotes a time in nature
when heaven seems to be on earth. Heaven
has placed itself beneath the earth, and so
their powers unite in deep harmony. Then
peace and blessing descend upon all living
things."*

I Cannot Hold Myself Close Enough

When I lie nose to nose with a flower,
one eye half clouded by the wetness of it all
my lips against the earth, sweet breath
of my body turning like the yellow that dresses
us both and my chest cold against the ground,
my arms are the root of God, spread
into the shape of flying;

Yes, there is tetanus in the grit between my teeth
and fifty years of pesticides born into my bones
bits of shell, the prehistoric homes of mollusk
and the sky could come crashing down at any moment
because who really knows anything but the feel
of cold, of dirt of damp the taste
of salt and iron scratched against the teeth
the deep sense that in all the beautiful, all
the terrible possibilities there comes a moment
called surrender.

12
P'I

Standstill [Stagnation]
*When Heaven and Earth are out of
communion all things are benumbed. There is
no meaningful relationship between internal
and external, so weakness predominates. The
inferior is ascending and depression prevails.*

promise

dark promise black promise promise made under capture
knife to ribs and arm twisted cracked toward the spine
bold promise loud promise promise i promise cross my
heart and hope to die *please let me die* promise promise
me i promise promise him i promise promise? fun
promise secret promise broken promise *broken heart* no
promise kept promise promise true and always promise
to be good.

13
T'UNG JEN
Fellowship with Men

*It is not selfish interest that creates
a fellowship, but attention to deeper goals and
universal concerns. If we look into our hearts
and make room openly for others, lasting
bonds are forged. Then we can undertake the
most difficult tasks and succeed.*

The Bloodheart Tree

If we forget our beginnings
we will never be at ease
will lose our wits as we stumble back
through endless aisleways of secret,
and things we don't forget.
You say, what if heaven is eternity
in the house of childhood?
but I say that denies the definition
of such a place.
The best thing is,
we can still laugh.
We take these horrors tenderly in our hands
one by one and carry them
like the dark and lustrous things they are
to the altar, place them
with our blessings
and light a candle for this place inside
we now call home.

Like the bloodheart tree outside your window
our own hearts become known to us
one reddening leaf at a time
bright and fragile in the snarl of common green.
If we know each other like this,
one unbelievable turning leaf at a time
even the future,
even if childless
and lived alone
makes sense.

your arms open
(that gift of trust from your parents),
you walk into the world and I
can hear your voice in the wind through
the bloodheart tree,
even when you do not call.

14
TA YU

Possession in Great Measure
*Strength draws clarity and they
unite. This is determined by destiny and
manifest through simple modesty. Here is
grace and the power behind it. Here is the
power of light; possession on a grand scale.*

And Then

I stuck my face into a flower it was
        wet like your eyes
        and as golden and I
moved my face over the

        cool surface as if it was
you I was caressing as if it
was you
growing here wild
among these stones.

15
CH'IEN
Modesty

The mountain is still. It is begot from the Creative, and is the quiet representative of Heaven on Earth. All modesty springs from a full and natural heart; thus the earth is cloaked in radiance.

A Greening

A dark green canopy of grape leaves, pale
curl of branches veining the trellis overhead,
this light filled field ahead of me
What does it mean to say green?
Gray green oak?
Lemon of new forsythia leaf?
Green purple of cosmos and buckwheat,
barley and rye?
What do I mean when I feel the greening of my heart
the way I feel your hand on my neck,
the sun on my shoulder,
the coarse stone of the wall we lean against?
There is a green of still waters that is like no other
humid and floating, reflective,
dappled with shadow and marsh grass, ducks
There is a green in the corner of my eye,
a place the brown lightens, as if even my body
is turning to reflect this greening world
Where does the green end and the gold begin?
the brown, and the blue?
Only the white clouds shout their separateness

and their longing.
The green intensifies as the sun moves back and forth
between the still white clouds, still clouds
sky and sun shifting behind them and the green
the green that burns to the left and right of me
then laughs its open-mouthed laugh to earth
as I pass by.

16
YU

Enthusiasm

*The best leaders adjust themselves to the
nature of their followers in order to create
enthusiasm. Nature itself moves along the line
of least resistance, and this tendency is
imminent in all living things.
"To know the seeds, that is divine indeed."*
— *Confucius*

This Garden

Each day it's a new garden.
Marigolds and mint duke it out
for the lions share of the redwood box
spicy carnations arch and spike
the scallop squash grows mutant,
a dark green zeppelin, ridged and splotched.
Who can say
how the seeds we plant will grow?
Gnarled, gray, stuck
in the ground eye-up the potatoes
become a ferny canopy, shade the peppers
bruise the dill
No one told me a zucchini bush could take-
over half a garden
Where there was a path yesterday, today
is a tangle of cantaloupe leaves
one tiny spaghetti squash dangles in the dark
center of a tomato plant taller than I am
and the morning glories insist on

climbing up the fence
instead of the trellis I labored over,
just as I insist on my own undirected life.
I pinch and tie and train but this garden
has a heart of its own, which it follows despite
my good wishes and knowing hand
So be it.
If the carrots are smothered by cucumbers
we shall live on less bright roots
take in the darker pith and skin of those
vining survivors and praise these stubborn lives
however they may grow.

17
SUI

Following

"Joy in movement induces following."
It is not necessary to understand where one is
going; one obtains a following and learns to
follow by listening carefully to the demands of
the time. Keep step with destiny and all goes
well.

Following

she shuts her eyes forms a bridge with her fingers leans
into a wall of winter light   the garden darkens with the
smell of roses and pine   darkens around her shoulders
as the last rays of sun illuminate the crown of her head
a single strand of hair escapes/floats in the salmon
colored sky

the sea slides his tongue along her body slides his hands
up her spine cradles her knees her elbows tucked into
the shape of a shell partly opened but dark inside   her
hair floats around her like the red petals of anemone
she moves the way she would beneath the hands of a
lover   just the lightest touch on her shoulder blade and
she knows which way to turn

summer is over now   the sand blows hard against the
building sculpts her coat around her stings her eyes
she feels the bend of her waist through her pocket
brushes the hair from her mouth thinks about the
people in the beach encampment living a place where
wall and roof merge to form a single curve   the quiet

place between breaths   each step leads to the next step
she doesn't know where she's going   she knows she's
going home

18
KU

Work on What Has Been Spoiled
[Decay]

"Rigid adherence to tradition has resulted in decay."

Beach

She was lying on her back. Al bent over her. And he saw the bright evening star reflected in her eyes, and he saw the black cloud reflected in her eyes. "We'll go on the train," he said. — John Steinbeck

but this is about things. keeping things. dragging things around in bags, pushing things in shopping carts, fighting over things that don't fit, that need an electrical outlet, that are broken. this is about belief and holding on and how these things make a home. how shoe laces that match can make a day. how a bag of rice swelled with rain water is still called *mine*. this is not about structures or warmth or family or a place to sleep that's the same every night. this is about things. about carrying, about holding. this is about sarge accusing victor of stealing his canned goods. about clutching a broken blue comb and a reel of fishing line that someone salvaged when they saw the plastic edge sticking out of the sand. this is about desire. this is about a playboy magazine lying open next to a beat up copy of the grapes of wrath open to a page about desire and about moving on. this is about going but it's not about going free it's about holding on to every step to every scrap to every broken-eyed doll and ragged piece of sweater. this is about winter storm and what it turns up. this is about furniture too heavy to move left strewn on the beach to reflect the mid-day light, one more shoe buried and the sound of waves.

19
LIN

Approach

Everything earthly is transitory, but that need not preclude a destined approach. Even though descent is sure to follow, when one has inner strength, awareness and consistency, approach brings good fortune.

Approach

the whole huge terrible beautiful body of you; your dark and resinous smell, sticky sweet tuberose and new mown hay, heavy air of the dog days of summer, your taupe colored skies that break for lightened salmon sunsets. I want to throw myself down on your damp green chest, press my heart to your heart, thick mud and living root, the broken tile and mildewed grout, crumbling facade and soot and yellowed air; the terrible violence of your heart blown open. I scrape my knuckles on you, bang my head against your filthy sweating streets and take you God; as angry as you are I look into your ferocious lovely face and I say yes to you. I lift my skirt, kick off my shoes and fall to my knees in one huge mouthed yes. I do this with no reason, just the off key alleluia of my life.

20
KUAN

Contemplation (View)
The subtlety of this hexagram lies in its double meaning. One becomes both the viewer and the viewed; the contemplator and the example for contemplation.

Contemplation

The doe bends her front legs and collapses like a folding chair. She is on my front lawn lying in the low, sparse grass chewing her cud. It is raining a fierce rain that rattles the gutters and slams at the windows and the doe lies there. I think she is watching me at the window as I watch her — perhaps she wonders if I can move through the glass. She has not eaten the garden trimmings I left outside the fence; broccoli full of aphids, browning tomatoes, crisp cucumber leaves and the end of year mums. I've often found her, nose to the wire, staring into the garden; but outside, the same green zucchini vines, one still with flower, prove distasteful. She is picky, prefers to mow down growing things. Who can blame her? What I find amazing is her calm. I am bundled in socks and sweaters, a hat, and even a muffler inside the house, a wild storm outside, and the doe leans back a bit in the grass; ears out like two propellers, eyes fastened on this window — on my face, or her own reflection — and chews her cud. It is bone cold, and wet, and a long-limbed, rib sharp doe lies in the grass like summer. At odds with myself, and restless, the best I can do is watch her as she shakes the rain off, chews, shakes. I envy that big-eared deer that simple shake. For her, it is only the rain.

21
SHIH HO
Biting Through

 噬嗑

Force is sometimes necessary to remove obstacles. The energetic snapping together of the teeth, indicated in nature by thunder and lightning, overcomes any disturbing tension that keeps one separate from others or from one's own heart.

Rise

I feel you rise in me
like the full blown moon
low on the horizon, rise
in me, like the sea
in an unexpected storm,
rise, then rise, like sun
over desert mountains
fringe of glowing light.
You rise, and my heart
becomes those mountains
dark and sharp in their ancient
language; becomes that glow.

If you are the sea,
I am sea life rising for air,
plankton floating, breaching whale
If you are earth,
then I am each seed cracking,
uncurling, reaching down, shooting
up to the visible sky.

Your sky makes me cloud
and lightning both, fog, white
blinding rain

You rise, like hands at a wedding,
like eyes in church and I become
that cathedral; buttressed,
solid as stone,
damp and cool and holy,
spirit and host.
I feel you rise in me
as bread rises, as bile rises
as brackish water floods sea gates;
and in the rising I become
those gates, and then that rising,
until the pressure cleaves me open
cleaves me whole.

22
PI

Grace

*It is fire that blazes, illumines and
beautifies the heavens. This fire is sparked in
the mineral depths of the earth. Grace —
beauty of form, which reflects this fire, is
necessary for life to be pleasing rather than
discordant.*

Metallurgy

Bright beacon
shining brow
deep cove and copper laughter
ringing golden sound
greening spirit gilds with light
and music, is gilded
in return
Your edge is tempered steel
finest silver
polished brass
cuts clean, a force
of nature
reflective and pure
You nourish
with mouth, with hands, your eyes
hold everything give everything away
You move forward now
unafraid into the ringing
resonance of your own
newly polished heart

You say you want the darkening
chords of cello
but when I listen for you
I hear the grace of bells.

23
PO
Splitting Apart

Inferior forces overcome the strong, not directly, but by way of secret passages and covert manipulation. This causes a split and eventually collapse. "Extreme caution is necessary in this isolation."

Don't Tell

at every instant when a collapse seems to occur, the entire universe is said to split into parallel worlds, each containing one of the possible outcomes of measurement. At every instant billions upon billions of such splits take place. There is no communication between these worlds. We cannot tell that we are constantly splitting into duplicate selves because our consciousness rides smoothly along only one path in the endlessly forking chains. — Barrow & Wheeler

So when my fingers find
the place
I whisper
'don't tell'
to the pillowcase
who holds my head together
like a lover should
who is sleeping
and I whisper
'don't wake him'
to the wall.

24
FU

Return (The Turning Point)
*Everything in nature returns, is born of
and lives within a cycle. In this way the world
constantly completes itself. Acceptance of this
allows one to come into the fullness of being at
the appropriate time.*

Return

I could look at that face, the same face, endlessly.
Almost cube-like auburn wings follow the line of
eyebrow, and the deep mouth, ripe like a fig. Her hands,
small animals themselves, rest on a counterpane, laced
and checked in odd design. A fetus engraved on a tear
shaped coin hangs over her shoulder and the gold foil
wall, its trees espaliered, flattens into a sheet of paper
fine enough to wrap a gift; or oneself, if it finally comes
to that.
She looks beyond me, clear as a moon — those eyes,
not green not blue, and I fall into her water, hand, foot
and knee, knowing when I emerge it will start all over,
will begin again. So I look at that face, the same face,
and wonder about capture and longing and lust; the
place the eye leaves off and the heart begins.

25
WU WANG

Innocence (The Unexpected)

*Spring is the time when life energy
is stimulated and begins to move, insisting
that everything blossom. Although this
happens year after year, it feels new each time
and is experienced with the innocence of youth;
as unintentional or unexpected.*

Innocence (The Unexpected)

Somewhere in sleep I cross that line and take you.
A man young enough to be my son; a boy really.
Lanky, with a tender face and hands that curve
as if they had no bone.
Our skin is the same color, our hair, our eyes,
some tribal memory sends me into you sleeping here
beside me, belted into the back seat of a car.
I look at you and want to feel my skin against your
skin, my hands rolling through your hair; want to
feel your new mouth on mine, feel this mouth, that
has tasted so many men, against the flat place of
your belly. I imagine the sounds you would make
as my face moved lower to capture you.
I want to kiss your ear and breathe lightly there
I think you've never felt that, or felt a woman's
long hair caress you as she slides her body down
the length of yours;
At the same time I want to stroke your face as if
you were my child, cradle you within this deep
erotic longing, as if you had somehow come from
my own body, somehow had nowhere else to go.

26
TA CH'U
The Taming Power of the Great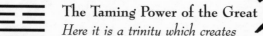

Here it is a trinity which creates
stability — three ways of 'holding firm':
holding together, holding back and holding to
care for and nourish.

Delicate

There is a delicate space that holds us
slides between us where my skin touches yours,
your skin, that reminds me of the air at morning,
rising light over the city, soft swell of disbelief.
Such delicate feeling, so delicate.
The delicate sound of our two erratic hearts
skipping beats against each other,
the space two hands make as they reach out,
the simple space between breaths
one whole room, safe, and without sound.
The fragile extra heart we create in all that percussive space
one heart, snapped in two, thickened with grief
and leaking in the dark-eyed long look back.
You shield your own widening heart,
your graceful hand held chest high;
hold yourself as long as you need
until that hand tunes, fine as glass, then shatters
like the original godhead
sending the great pained protected battered heart of you
into all things, which can hold you, the way
the music holds you
in all its delicate deepening sound

and as I hold you, lightly, with gratitude for all
you are not and are.

27

I

The Corners of the Mouth
(Providing Nourishment)

*Nourishment here is both of the body and of
the spirit. This leads to the idea of caring for
and nourishing others as well as oneself.*

Corners of the Mouth

Only parsnips remain in the soaking garden.
I hesitate to pull them up, they are a winter
talisman, the luck that anchors growth
to growth, across this year and that.
Perhaps the lucent spears will knuckle and spoil,
toughen, or hollow like some great ancient tomb
upon whose narrow walls we will read notes to ourselves
buried long ago.
Maybe frost will moisten and sweeten them instead;
neither charms nor words, they await their perfect death
ready, with the soil still clinging to their fine,
innumerable hairs, ready, warm and buttered
to feed us through the long cold; simple
the story they have grown to tell.

28
TA KUO

Preponderance of the Great
*The weight of the great is excessive,
unsupportable. In such times one must take
as an example the tree, which stands firm even
though it is solitary, and joy, which carries on
even if it must renounce the world.*

Madrone

Beautiful red-blood heart of madrone
curls through the center of a years dead log
it is a voice we see in the effort to cleave
such a raw and savage thing from its forest life;
It will make a fire and we will be glad.

I am told that madrone trees hate change,
and people; they die for no reason, not bugs
not rot, just sensitive red heart.

29
K'AN
The Abysmal (Water)

坎

Water flows on, following its own essential nature. This is its power. In situations of danger or difficulty, one does best to act like water; remain true under all conditions. With a sincere heart, it is possible to penetrate the meaning of any situation.

Dungeness, Yesterday

Strange like birds
a constant motion
the sound of water over stones
   of hollow bones
   and refuge
where things go from large to
small
   then smaller
to nothing   and   nothing
again.
A woman collects beach rocks,
lines them up on swollen driftwood,
soaks her shoes
her hair   everything
turns to look at the same
time;
the water
never stops sighing.

30
LI

≡≡

The Clinging, Fire

Fire takes its form from the source that feeds it. It flames up only when it has something to cling to. So it is with the soul, which becomes luminous when it finds something persevering within itself as nourishment.

The Clinging, Fire

The big digging is over.
Jewelers pick and brush,
delicate hands of archaeologist,
the sour taste of saliva and trust.

I am gathering back the strands of myself.
Drawing them into the space two hands make,
rubbing them together,
waiting for the flame to rekindle.

31
HSIEN

≡≡
≡≡

Influence (Wooing)

The heart may lead, so the body follows.
Words, too, become meaningless if there is no
heart behind their movement.

咸

Influence (Wooing)

Since I have lost my language, my body has to speak. It
feels free to desire you as deeply as it does; to admit the
rush of blood that fills me when I think of you. I can
hardly stand myself; how engorged my tissues feel, how
wet I am, how much I want your hands on me, your full
sweet mouth and your eyes on me, your deep pained
eyes.

I can barely contain this constant moan and when I
touch myself, when I make myself come to release the
pressure of you growing inside me and all over me, I
wonder if you can feel the shock waves all the way across
the plains.

How long can this go on? Perhaps time will drift you
out of my memory, blunt this longing; but what to do?
All this love, all this wanting and no words.

32
HENG

Duration

"Duration is a state whose movement is not worn down by hindrances." This is not standstill, but self-renewing movement that is subject to natural law. Like breath, an ending is reached through inhalation, but always a new beginning follows with the outward reach of exhalation. This duration, in its various forms, is the basis of life.

Duration

It is always gnawing on the edges of things; gums, fingers. It leaves me dreamless and sucks the center out of desire. I wake in its arms each morning and before the acid edge cuts my stomach I know it's there. It's not happy or unhappy, it doesn't press for tears or make the battery go dead. It is like the half eye-lid of a lizard, the thin web spun round a fly; a cotton-candy-like vagueness. If I squeeze it between my fingers it gets more dense, but just a drop of water and it melts to nothing. It is not the lump in the throat, the weight on the chest or the cramp in the abdomen. It is not the light smeared under the lip of the shade. It is not the rank taste pooling the corners of my mouth, it is not longing. I did not catch it from anyone, cannot will it away. It is a part of me; like the hole in my heart, the single horseshoe kidney, my restlessness, impatience. Sometimes it is as subtle as the wind lifting a hair on my arm. Other times it binds like a twisted slip. When it's cold like this I almost welcome its presence. It keeps me pressed to the bed, pinned at the wrists like a lover might. But there is no play here. This is dead serious; like a mother's panicked yelling, like a rope around my neck — expecting a fall.

33
TUN

Retreat

When the power of the dark overwhelms, withdrawal
is the appropriate response. Retreat is sometimes
the only way to keep from exhausting one's forces.
"In what is small, perseverance furthers."

The Particular Smell of Death
Nadine Apartments 1987–1988

John tells me there is a certain smell to death.
It is the same with everyone.
I sleep on the couch, smell my own breath
heavy on the pillow;
it is the same with everyone,
each of us in our own small room.
Some of us grow narcissus in bowls on the table,
Dave keeps a cat, Merit has never
gotten her stove to heat right,
she has to set it on broil to bake a cake;
but she's learned the system now,
what to give and how much to take.
Often we sit in the halls, let other people
talk to us, then retreat to our rooms to find
a moth beating its wings against the window
blind, liquid yellow track light, a man
asleep under the bush outside.
Tonight the first floor tenants
are having a party; I've decided to type.
John is upstairs studying about death,
you know, cells and things;
but you just can't put that smell in a book.

34
TA CHUANG
The Power of the Great

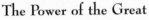

*There is an overwhelming power in the upward
moving energy of spring. It is a wild
movement, but is in accord with Heaven, so it
enhances all that comes within its bounds.*

Lavender

As I water the garden I notice how each plant exposes
her heart, opens her legs in empathy with my own
opening; shows off the deepest part of herself as if to say
take me, come take me.
What before I would have called *ranginess,* or *untidy
growth habit,* I now glory in. What in me wanted those
perfectly manicured rounds of golden thyme when I
could have open-hearted red stemmed long legged lilac
flowered wildness all around me?
And the fragrance...
Everything is copulating or longing for it; bees and
butterflies crowd the lavender, box elder beetles scuttle
backwards attached at the abdomen. I cannot keep my
hands off my own breasts. My heart strains to crack
these bones and find its bloody mate. I want nothing
but hands on me, nothing but to please and be pleased.
I want a man so deep inside me that everything tears,
that this uncircumcised heart is ripped open finally;
makes covenant with God.
I am wild with desire and even the plants in my garden
respond, languid in the June heat but reaching, it seems,
to brush me as I pass.

A wisteria tendril catches my own loose hair, snags me back for a moment; the scent of woolly thyme is newly erotic and the lavender — I want bunches of it up me, I want to gather it until I cannot move for the holding.

35
CHIN

Progress

The lifting of the sun as it rises is a symbol for widening clarity. It illuminates everything that was previously hidden by dark mists. This makes for easy progress.

Hands

there were always fingers in her hair
they seemed to be caught there and pulled
at the tangles that were natural in that place
no eyes or focus just hands and a long white belly
hands and a smooth space to ride against
the wind could make fingers be hands
it knew how and her hair slid like a place
no hands had been before
her hair wove dark sky dark hands that lifted
her from a language that no longer had a smell
she was fragrant here and the hills
became the body of the lover she had waited for
curled here inside herself beneath a skin
now open to all its water.

36

MING I

Darkening of the Light

The sun sinks beneath the earth. All is darkened. This "wounding of the bright" holds true for the heart as well and one must remain persevering to overcome the difficult time.

Darkening of the Light

It is dark and it holds the sound of the night-time train as a cup holds water. Just enough and always where she can find it. Just open a door and it becomes a light around the edge. Find it at the nape crawling with the fingerprints of this or that lover that left their mark; the smudge on the linoleum that got ground in and won't bleach out anymore. She feels it like a bad knee in the rain, an ache that lingers, a stiffness in her voice. Her hair feels too heavy on her head. The lines blur before she can steady the pen. The books and all the angles she's developed and practiced and perfected that press her forward even when all she wants is to scream stop it stop it make me stop it. And sitting in the movie she thinks will I be depressed again when it's over and I have to clear the calendars and move the furniture and meet people smiling and dirty and drive and drive and pray for rain and a new novel and a new fantasy to escape to in the night. Her hair smells like cigarette smoke and she's tired and it's sweet dark and thank god no one can save her at last.

CHIA JEN
The Family [The Clan]

家人

"The foundation of the family is the relationship between husband and wife. The tie that holds the family together lies in the loyalty and perseverance of the wife."

The Family

This downtown corner wasn't so different twenty years ago. Maybe this is where he met her; dirty white buildings, bus exhaust and the smell of new tar in the air. Three o'clock I would just be coming home from school, my mother in the living room ironing in her bra and trousers, my sister already playing in the cul-de-sac. What was she like? What color lipstick did she wear? Was she dark like us, or blond, sophisticated and smart? How did he touch her? Did he take out the false front teeth before he kissed her, the way he took them out each night when he walked through our door? Would he set them on the nightstand next to the full ashtray and his deck of cards? Did he undress her, or did he watch as she pulled the black slip up over her head, her arms slightly flabby and pale? Or was she young and stupid, a kid impressed with his intelligence and broad forehead? Was she the one who wore the cheap gold earring my mother found on the floor of his car? Maybe she looked like my mother, my mother who never said a word but chewed her anger as she listened secretly to phone conversations from the other room. Did he know her long, her, I mean, was it a *her*? Did she matter to him?

Did she come to his funeral? Did she know how he
died? Did she go home to water african violets, make
instant coffee and watch TV? My brother asked me,
'can you blame him?' But my question is 'what did he
want?' Here was my mother, angry and ironing and me,
silent as stone and my sister, running. Here was the
furniture he chose in the house he built at the far end
of the suburbs. Here was his naugahyde chair, my
perfect grades, the meal cooked every night that my
sister and I ate alone. Here we were in this home he
created taking whatever he would give us and if he was
God as I was told in so many silent ways then why
didn't he want us?

38
K'UEI

Opposition

"Often it seems to a man as though everything were conspiring against him. He sees himself checked and hindered in his progress, insulted and dishonored."

睽

But My Name is Allan

you got some pretty hair
I like the way it blows in the wind — some guy

Just give me some time and I can get used to anything. Even these boys that walk around with their high tops untied, the way she drops my pen four times on the asphalt until it only writes every other letter, or the way they always talk to her, even when she's on my arm and here she is dropping my pen and they're talking to her like who am I?

It's a Tuesday and the clocks got turned so now instead of sitting inside drinking a beer and watching something on the tube we're out here, at the beach, looking at the sun turn orange, then more orange then, plop, it'll be gone. Just like that. And I won't even get the green flash that I saw in the film at the Museum of Science and Industry. She always makes me go to the films. I like the coal mine. But she thinks this boardwalk is romantic. Look at this place; it's filthy, people rolled up in blankets on the sidewalk, dog shit everywhere, whole place smells like pizza. This guy in a cape is following us and talking to her and she's laughing. I kick another can onto the bike path. I wish that goddamn sun would drop already. Then it'll get dark and all of a sudden it'll be scary and she'll get cold and we can go home.

39
CHIEN

Obstruction

Adversity is fundamental for self-development because it throws a person back upon herself. So a short-lived obstruction, tackled with unswerving inner purpose, brings good fortune in the long run.

Obstruction

This is the sense of things
the experience only body knows
a circling wind through the palo verde
blue of a foreign sky
the weight of head on neck
bite of pepper, pinch of pain, pounding
of this uncontrollable blood.
The pull of the world is stronger than emotion
It asks us to carry this extra body,
this head, the one we've wrestled with
all our lives; that angel of memory
And we are left with a broken hip, even
as we prevail, it is we who carry the scar
into our triumph, we who have been
broke open and left exhausted to carry on.
It doesn't matter what we know, the body
requires a kind of pain, a longing that
becomes its compass, shaves clean the skin
of history and regret that holds us to a place,
asks us to look back, gain widening perspective.
It stalls, cracks bone and fortune alike,

then like a river passed its ford or yellow
wind, finally releases us, sweeps us
broken, but laughing, into a brand new sky.

40
HSIEH

Deliverance

Sudden change has a powerful influence. Like rain, which breaks atmospheric tension "making all the buds burst open," deliverance from emotional pressure is both liberating and enlivening.

Deliverance

Kissing you

is like breathing
after having been under water
for a long, long time.

41
SUN

Decrease

*Increase and decrease come and go.
Decrease does not always indicate poverty of
spirit. What is crucial is to avoid empty
pretense, to admit insecurities as well as the
deeper sentiments of the heart; to be
unashamed of simplicity.*

Decrease

there is a light that shines off your eyelid as if it knew
the green inside required yellow to make it whole. and
the tender line your knee makes against its own shadow.
there is a triangle of mauve caught between your legs
and it darkens as the sun does, the crease across your
forehead deepens like your eyes and the tree cuts the sky
into your name.
it doesn't matter that you don't love me. doesn't matter
at all. these feelings that swell in my chest, between my
legs, are mine and the earth calls me down when you're
here, when you're not.
o god. really. listen. it doesn't matter, does it?

42

I

Increase

During this enriched time, even those things that seem unfortunate take on a positive aspect and become advantageous. One who acts in harmony with the time is free of error and exerts a powerful influence on those around her.

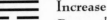

Increase

and when she understood that she would never bear a child, something inside her broke loose, became a field of longing turned outward. She fell in love with everyone she passed, wanting to touch their sleeve, their arm, their hand, pull them to her breast, lean into the wall of their body. Not yet desire, she could not stop it; gathering strands of cool hair in her curling fingers she felt the gray in it, the brittle lightness it had become. There was a tender spot at the cleft of her back — that, and her ribs would not line up straight, but rubbed and crossed, clicking in the deepest part of night. She thought she would dry up, but instead she became fuller; her body a lush flesh and ever present blood that blushed her skin the pink of an infant's ear and called to her each time it crossed her heart, called her home.

43
KUAI

Break-through (Resoluteness)
*Becoming entangled with our own faults
in hatred and passion serves no purpose in
self-development. Instead, we must accept our
own shortcomings and be on guard against
their insurgence without combating them
directly. Thus their weapons become dulled.*

Acceptance

a tiny coil; smaller than an i.u.d. or a clock spring or an
eyelash, finer than a spider leg, a spider web, a breath.
curled inside amidst the fear and pain and confusion,
but glowing. sometimes it slithers up her spine and
makes her hot; other times it lays twisted like a breech
baby, makes her howl with the effort to turn it. she feels
it rise pale and golden like the last spoon of winter sun,
the shimmer of gas heat, a bone, a shade, a shard of
glass. it is as yellow as oil, as slick as teeth, it lifts like a
cap from her head in an unexpected wind. she is not
sorry. it hurts. it hurts and still she is not sorry. she is
alive.

44
KOU

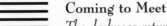

Coming to Meet
The darkness returns unexpectedly.
"Of its own accord the female principle comes
to meet the male." This creates a dangerous
situation which we must understand to prevent
possible unhappy consequences.

Coming to Meet

It was morning and the difference was striking. He had
never seen her like this before, so soft and open. He
struck a match against the table edge and watched the
flame reflect in the dark of her eyes. Her hands lay still
in her lap, palms up and fingers curled slightly. She was
talking, very quietly. He just watched the flame move
down until it almost burned his fingers then he shook it
out, a game he played as a child. She kept talking, not
trying to draw him in, but talking more softly so he had
to lean forward now to hear her. Everything about her
seemed transparent, even her dark lashes took on the
quality of spider web after a rain. He could see himself
in her eyes, a perfect mirror. He felt his heart move to
the back of his body as she revealed herself, his throat
close. He could take her in his hands right now and
snap the life out of her. It would be that easy. Then he
could breathe again, close his eyes. But he didn't move.
Just leaned against his knees and ran his tongue along
the ridge of his teeth. She had no right to see him so
clearly and stay. No right. It made him want to kill her.

45
TS'UI

Gathering Together [Massing]
This is not time for arbitrary choice.
Secret forces are pulling together those who
belong together; our job is to yield to this
attraction. "Where inner relationships exist, no
great preparations and formalities are
necessary."

Adrift

I am set adrift by you
deep onto the sea of my own bruised heart
Each kiss, the way your hand
traces the fine bone of my hip, your hair
like some smoky halo flaming and floating
around your head, above our ferocious bodies
our tender mouths
Just the thought of you
like a new green river freshly cutting
its rocky banks opens me
Put your hand on me. there.
And pull me into your own swelling sea
swirling with the heart of you, large
as a mountain, just as still

46
SHENG

Pushing Upward

*This is a growth associated with great
effort; just as plants use all their energy for
pushing upward through the earth. Here,
success is associated with force of will.*

Pushing Upward

Hot green smell of sun on pine,
the apple tree full of bees
pink blossomed, humming sound
frothy white lilac heads
above the crayon green of this April
and the tulips, graceful, hang on.
Everything is so delicate
and righteous, so human in regard
beneath unseasonal sun; the lilac
flowers, each one perfectly four sided,
box elder beetles running as they mate,
the curling hat of lettuce, unripe
peas wishing for weather, swelling.
Each thing confronts its death daily
in its will to grow;
midday sun wilts the radish leaf,
tulip petals brown and curl, dust
the ground with fine yellow talc
violets, pink lamium, insect bitten
laurel leaf and the purple flowering
adjuga spikes, lavender thyme, fennel,
tansy, the willful horseradish and fat

gray wisteria buds, naked and terrible,
trembling, ready to burst with just
one more day of sun.
An offshore breeze ruffles blue bellied
borage, hairy podded poppies, violas
and weeds.
I worry about the hole in the ozone,
but the round pink radish grows to flesh
from seed, spindly peppers push tiny
heads through the crusty earth, uncurl,
and make themselves known;
a surprise, each time.
Each day is an act of faith, each hour,
each moment, each bud.

47
K'UN

Oppression (Exhaustion)
Here the image is of a dried up lake, of
exhaustion. It is a dark line holding down two
light lines, a light line trapped between two
dark. All in all, the superior is restrained by
the inferior, creating an insecure position.

Coming to Terms: Love

When I speak of love
I do not mean the dark rooms
of the heart,
but the constant shifting
of hands and feet
the nervous scrambling
for the next hold.

48
CHING
The Well

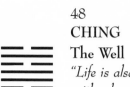

"Life is also inexhaustible. It grows neither less nor more; it exists for one and for all."

Splitting Wood

Curly grained and auburn,
each wedge falls from the maul
a testament to winter
and the endlessness of life.

This is why I love splitting wood;
you can't see the heart of things
until you cut them.

49
KO

Revolution (Molting)

*The light and dark forces struggle; this
causes the revolution of the seasons. We can
master these changes and learn to keep our
balance by understanding their regularity and
cyclic nature. Then, what appears chaotic
becomes clear, and we are able to adjust.*

What the Body Gives Us

The spring never comes soon enough, or stays long
enough or is pure enough or green enough except after
the disaster when there is too much water with no place
to go and the earth sucks it up and we find earthworms
crawling across the sidewalk eating the particles/eating
the death. And what we want is to go home to a good
dinner and a warm bed and hours where we don't have
to be awake and don't think about waking up again.
Sometimes I go so fast the telephone wires string my
dreams and tie them off right before the surgeon cuts
them and makes me sterile and is gone. And in the
spring the animals lose their sacks and they continue in
the world empty for longing, but they never understand
how they arrive; like the children from Zeus's head, like
the light from Paul's head, like the head we carry
beneath our arm, shading the face from other stares.
It still amazes me that we can pass through such small
holes, tunnel through such fierce fire, look up without
losing our balance, without falling off the edge and grasp
again, what the body gives us.

50

TING

The Cauldron

Wood nourishes flame and becomes a
symbol for the spirit. All that is visible must
extend to the invisible, where it is clarified and
becomes consecrated. Like the tree that
provides the wood, the soul is thus able to take
root in the cosmic order.

The Cauldron

The air is full of pins today, gnats and sun and allergy,
biting flies. But my thoughts lay on the clean blue plate
of the world like a perfect meal, just the one I wanted
and mine alone.

I am thinking of longing, the deep green feel of a man
so high inside me I can't tell where our edges end, or
meet for that matter. And I wonder if that will ever be
mine again, and if not, what kind of container will I
become? And how will I survive? Can I become like
Hildegaard of Bingen, walking through the fields in deep
desire, wanting the great hand of God on her breast, but
holding that desire; like the question that does not want
an answer, that backs away from the small climax each
death makes.

If desire is the question, is satisfaction the answer; the
end of that road? Or can this walk across Wisconsin
fields so filled with my own longing that I cannot speak
be enough? Can the hunger grow so filling that it leaves
no room for substance, turns even solid want sublime?

51
CHEN

The Arousing (Shock, Thunder)
*"There are three kinds of shock — the
shock of heaven, which is thunder, the shock
of fate, and finally, the shock of the heart."*

The Arousing

Time is changing shape.
This winter it has become long
and very thin, almost invisible,
It has slipped right by me
where I sit, caught between two flames
waiting for the call to leap,
like the painting of St. Augustine
his hand flung out in sharp surprise
to grasp a luminous heart whose fire
halos his head as well, his own
deep thoughts and eyes, startled
at God's hard joke.

Time is flexible, like body parts
that shove and shift, make room for
new life which grows; and if this means
the heart must flee through the smallest
slit, some saintly hand will snatch it,
will hold it up and out, shining
with the fire of unknowing, shaped
by the holy teeth of ghosts.

52
KEN

Keeping Still, Mountain

*Only when one has attained inner calm
can she turn to the outside world without
becoming entangled in struggle and tumult. It
takes this true peace of mind to understand
the laws of the universe and act in accord with
them.*

Keeping Still, Mountain

with only the green smell of pine
dark in my nostrils
and salt of my own skin
I sit in the night garden;
listen to flowers move.

53
CHIEN

Development (Gradual Progress)
*Just as a tree develops, slowly, and from
the root, so should we develop in accord with
our truest nature; gradually, step by step. In
this way we stand firmly rooted. Deep inside
is tranquility, which guards us; without is
penetration, which makes progress possible.*

Bare

winter trees
a great sea we dive into
as this road curves down from a crest,
the pure language of ash-
colored branches scratches the sky, this nudity
tears at me in a place I'm rarely torn;
an elemental place not my own.

I have always loved the bones of things, the naked
brittle truth, which even as it cuts
begins a healing,
clean sews the rend our coupling makes
leaves etched a scar as delicate
as winter trees against a fading sky, dead-
seeming things —
but deep inside sap swells, green with waiting
bides time as only plant
life can, next spring
it clothes a forest.

54
KUEI MEI

The Marrying Maiden
*"But every relationship between
individuals bears within it the danger
that wrong turns may be taken, leading to
endless misunderstandings and disagreements.
Therefore it is necessary constantly to remain
mindful to the end."*

The Marrying Maiden

with no responsibility
for that small life or your hard cock
you want to make a baby and listen to it breathe
'that's the way I wish it was' you say
and send me out to plant turnips
and squash what we share with victims
who only know our names and shine
the hidden sorrow nightly with their sleeves.

55
FENG

≡≡

Abundance [Fullness]
*If clarity is within, and movement
without, one has greatness and abundance.*

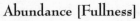

Is Enough

birds sit on the tree
outside my window

like the last persimmons
of winter
beautiful fruit.

56
LU

The Wanderer

As a wanderer has no permanent home, and is married to the road, she must be careful to remain upright and honorable. In this way she "sojourns only in the proper places."

旅

The Wanderer

Your mouth itself becomes two bodies
separated by a long, undulating horizon.
Like the earth and the sky, like you and me.
— Man Ray

We are drawn by the same force;
a thin thread of ambition to be alone
with the road, with the movie of our lives
verdant and without horizon, littered
with houses and people, broken hearts,
and the last large intake of the widening sky.

If it is eyes, they see, and hands move
as if they had a life of their own
still, this string pulls us,
not like a child pulls a toy;
moves us, not like a puppeteer moves
his marionette — not a pencil drawing line,
or the curve of our understanding, or
the shape of our hearts,
but like the line of horizon defines a day
makes a lip for the world, whose mouth
speaks the voice of heaven.

57
SUN
The Gentle
(The Penetrating, Wind)

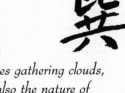

*In nature, the wind disperses gathering clouds,
leaving the sky clear. It is also the nature of
wind to create dust storms, making it difficult
to see. At such times it is small, penetrating
actions that have influence — this clarity of
judgment sweeps the sky of hidden motives.*

Wind

I spend my morning
beneath the rusty trees
sweeping the stones path
to my home
It is very pleasant this
   swish . swish
the wheat straw makes
slow work
       asks nothing of me.
    leaves . wrappers . sand
      bits of bread & droppings
       all sweep together
with dead caterpillars
a few ants   some pebbles
I make several small piles
a little family
move them closer & closer
until their edges are forgotten
& only contour reminds me

how they came together.
Some days the
lantern gate swings

    new wind
rattles my windows
scatters my sweeping
sends me hurrying
       inside
before the dust
blinds me
and I lose the path.

58
TUI

The Joyous, Lake

A self-contained joy wants nothing, is utterly content. It is without egotistic likes and dislikes and abides in the quiet security of a simple heart. This is the freedom that leads to good fortune.

The Joyous

A bird calls *sweet sweet* in the thin yellow air
dry yellow branches of palo verde blossom
pale and paler near the sound of a fountain
that moistens the lip of a hill
It is the delicate green bark of tree I long for
the absence of longing, nourishment taken
yearly through the root, this long yellow hair
that tints the sky like a halo to the edges of tree
a slow burning fire that stands in relief
against an otherwise cool sky; such wordless joy
This bird calls *sweet sweet* from the cradle
of a palo verde tree, his simple song the only one
he has, with which he calls forth the world.

59
HUAN

Dispersion [Dissolution]
"In the autumn and winter, water begins to freeze into ice. When the warm breezes of spring come, the rigidity is dissolved, and the elements that have been dispersed in ice floes are reunited. It is the same with the minds of the people."

Dispersion [Dissolution]

and seeing her ex-husband through the window, folding shirts in the low lights of the closed shop, she felt happy. he looked good. better than he ever had when they were together. his face didn't seem to hang at the corners so much. he had even grown a beard like she'd always wanted. she tapped on the window and waved. he smiled and made a silly gesture, trying to sell her the shirt he had in his hand. then she laughed and walked on. that's all it took she thought, a few years, some window. she couldn't remember, didn't even recognize the easy smile he gave. it was a part of him hidden to her all the years they ate and slept together. a small gift on a summer evening. a split second when the glass between them could dissolve.

60
CHIEH

Limitation

It is true that in life there are limitations. These often create boundaries between people and within the self.

Sunday Afternoon

That wet green smell
right after it's mown
the dads in their bermuda shorts
pot bellies, the particular
slump of their shoulders
and curl of barbecue smoke
hum and buzz of gnats that shimmer
on summer air and the family
down the street, the happy one
no one really knows.

61
CHUNG FU
Inner Truth

*Only an awakened heart that is free
of prejudice can be open to truth. Then the
visible effects of the invisible can manifest.*

中孚

Inner Truth

we have been asleep
for a long time now
because awake
means alone
no one to follow
or to carry
nothing important to put on

just face
movement
die

62

HSIAO KUO

Preponderance of the Small 小過

Here the weak mediates with the outside world and those in authority are by nature inadequate for the job. Actions have become empty form and need to be recombined with personal dignity in order to become correct.

Preponderance of the Small

the way men empty their pockets at night.
throw the change on a dresser, hang the keys
unfold bits of paper, scraps with numbers,
lunch receipts. each day same thing pockets
empty pockets full. pockets empty. the way
solar dust is sucked into black holes. the way
women empty their hearts into waiting pockets
wind up on a dresser with some change.

63
CHI CHI

After Completion
"Do not throw yourself away on the world but wait tranquilly and develop your personal worth by your own efforts."

既濟

Shears

lines of rain
cut the sky
make it
very still as if
someone took
huge ice shears
sliced out a chunk
just like that
a perfect square

and there we are
holding our breath
waiting for the
surface to melt
and someone to find us.

64
WEI CHI
Before Completion

It is spring, and we are led out of the stillness of winter into a fragrant blossoming. Now we must look closely at the nature of the life force to understand the proper place of all things.

Lilac

The lilac follows the daffodils and the fruit
blossoms, the camellias and the pale new leaves.
The town is full of lilac one morning. All
of a sudden, one day it is lilac; purple lilac,
white lilac, lilac so pale it is almost pink.
and I notice it like I notice the crinkled apple
blossoms, the peeling apricot bark and the tiny
partridges skirting a pile of tree prunings.
Even in the night it is lilac, the scent intensifies
then; lilac, and frenzied moths hitting the moist
lighted windows. I imagine every light is sky
to them, as they throw themselves, wings outspread,
into the hard sides of God.